MW01703180

Launching Your Accounting Career
A Step-by-Step Guide

Melanie McKay, PhD
Loyola University New Orleans

Elizabeth Rosa, MBA, CPA, CMA
DeSales University

THOMSON
CUSTOM PUBLISHING

Editor: Michele Baird
Production Coordinator: Lisa Donahue
Marketing Coordinator: Sara L. Hinckley

Printed in the United States of America

Thomson Learning Custom Publishing
5191 Natorp Blvd.
Mason, Ohio 45040
USA

For information about our products, contact us:
1-800-355-9983
http://www.custom.thomsonlearning.com

International Headquarters
Thomson Learning
International Division
290 Harbor Drive, 2nd Floor
Stamford, CT 06902-7477
USA

UK/Europe/Middle East/South Africa
Thomson Learning
Berkshire House
168-173 High Holborn
London WCIV 7AA

Asia
Thomson Learning
60 Albert Street, #15-01
Albert Complex
Singapore 189969

Canada
Nelson Thomson Learning
1120 Birchmount Road
Toronto, Ontario MIK 5G4
Canada
United Kingdom

Visit us at www.e-riginality.com and learn more about this book and other titles published by Thomson Learning Custom Publishing

ISBN 0-759-31649-X

The Adaptable Courseware Program consists of products and additions to existing Custom Publishing products that are produced from camera-ready copy. Peer review, class testing, and accuracy are primarily the responsibility of the author(s).

THE ACCOUNTING PROFESSION: A WORLD OF OPPORTUNITIES

The accounting profession has changed so dramatically since the mid-twentieth century that the variety of opportunities available to accounting majors today did not exist just a few decades ago. Changes in the corporate workplace, brought on by restructuring, globalization, and fast-developing information technology, have redefined the role of accountants in all phases of business.

As computers have replaced humans in "crunching the numbers," the traditional responsibilities of accountants—to gather and record information, to prepare financial statements, to monitor the financial results of operations, to audit and verify financial information, to prepare tax statements—have expanded.

In today's business environment, accountants are involved not only in these activities but also in financial analysis and management, business and technology consulting, e-commerce, strategic planning and decision support, performance measurement, process re-engineering and design, cross-functional teamwork, and many other activities.

Careers in Public Accounting

Public accountants work in firms that have traditionally provided financial accounting and audit services to businesses as well as tax preparation assistance to businesses and individuals. These firms range from one-person offices to the large multinational organizations that employ thousands of accountants. Now that even the smallest companies have their own computer systems to keep the books and generate financial statements, however, public accountants are focused less on statement preparation than on business planning and consulting.

Public accounting firms now advise clients on such matters as employee compensation and benefits, investment planning, accounting software selection, and design and maintenance of accounting information systems. Public accountants also work in such specialties as forensic accounting (the investigation of bankruptcies) and fraud investigation.

And, while today's public accountants still perform audits, this function now involves more than simply auditing a company's financial statements; it also includes auditing the organization's computer systems and performing other assurance services.

What's a CPA? The most highly prized professional credential of the public accounting profession is that of the CPA, or certified public accountant. The CPA is earned by passing the rigorous Uniform Certified Public Accountant Exam and by gaining work experience as an accountant. (Precise work experience requirements vary somewhat from state to state.) The combination of an accounting degree and the CPA credential will give you clout as you progress along your career path.

Careers in Private Accounting

Private accountants work in businesses and corporations. Private accountants gather financial information, prepare financial statements, and provide input into budget planning and cost control. They may also serve as internal auditors, evaluating their companies' accounting and other systems, looking for accuracy in record-keeping and reporting, and rooting out inefficiencies.

The role of private accountants has also expanded in recent years; rather than simply providing numbers and spreadsheets to management, these accountants now serve as integral members of most companies' strategic management teams. They work with professionals from engineering, marketing, and other areas in planning, product and project development, re-engineering, and other strategic activities.

Because management accountants are uniquely positioned not only to understand all phases of an organization's business but also to appreciate the ways in which the financial function intersects with marketing, information systems, engineering, production, and other functional areas, they are important members of the cross-functional teams companies create to initiate new projects, launch new products, and acquire major assets. Management accountants are frequently called upon to present recommendations to top management for improvement of systems, proposals for capital expenditures, and projects for global expansion.

Accounting Degree = Career Choices

Whether you've already decided to major in accounting or are taking your first accounting course, remember that a degree in accounting can be the ticket to a wide range of opportunities in management, finance, business consulting, government work, the nonprofit sector, and the arts. Whether you want to practice public accounting independently or work in a huge corporation, whether you like to analyze information, develop projects, advise clients, or implement computer systems, an accounting major can lead you to the career that's right for you.

Getting Started on Your Career

With the variety of options open to accounting majors, it is important for you to think about possible career choices early. This guide will help you begin charting your career path in your freshman year, find internships and summer jobs during your sophomore and junior years, target your first job as you approach graduation, get your foot in the door with prospective employers, and land the job you want.

Using the guide, you will learn how to:

- Explore the career options the accounting profession offers
- Obtain internship experience during your undergraduate years
- Research and identify your first job
- Prepare winning résumés and application letters
- Make a great impression on your interview
- Handle follow-up like a professional

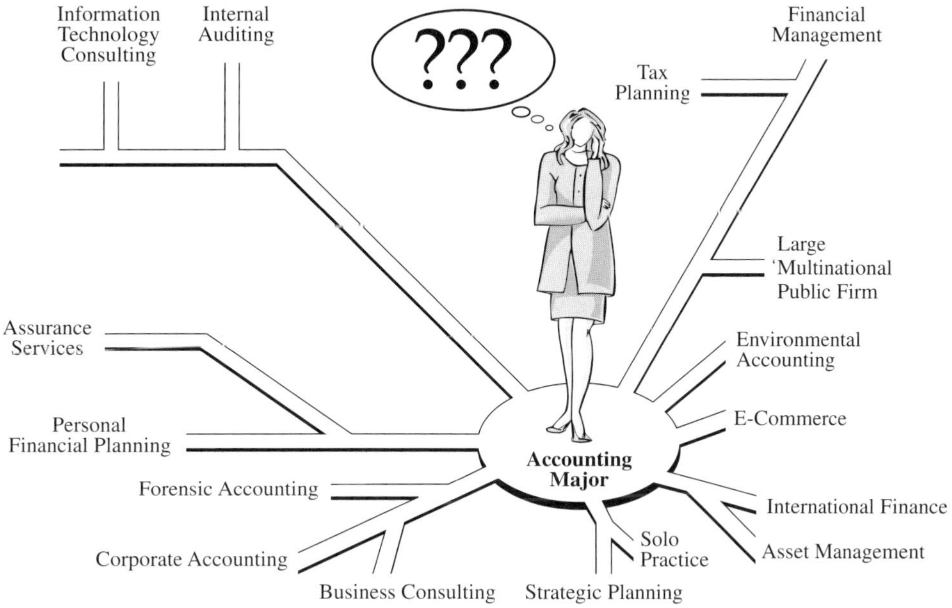

EXPLORING THE ACCOUNTING PROFESSION

Figure 1—Exploring Your Career Options

To take the first step on your career path, you need to explore the career options that an accounting major offers. Getting a clear picture of the profession requires research—on the Web, in professional and trade publications, on-site at firms and companies, in conversations on the phone and face-to-face with people working in accounting. Here are some suggestions for researching the accounting profession.

The Occupational Outlook Handbook This handbook, published by the U.S. Bureau of Labor, is the best place to begin general research on any career field. Available on-line (http://www.bls.gov/oco/ocos001.htm), the keyword "accountant" calls up career paths such as "accountants and auditors," "financial managers," "financial analysts and personal financial advisors," and "tax examiners." Each one of these "hits" contains information on types of jobs, required qualifications, nature of the work and working conditions, employment outlook, training, salary ranges, related occupations, and sources of additional information.

Recommendation for Action Go on-line to the *Occupational Outlook Handbook.* Find answers to the following questions:

1. Into what categories is the accounting profession divided?
2. How does the work of public accountants differ from that of private accountants?
3. How has computer technology changed the accounting profession?
4. What is a forensic accountant?
5. What new career paths are accountants expected to take in the next decade?
6. What is the growth prediction for jobs in accounting by the year 2010?
7. Which three career paths described in the *OOH* interest you most?

<u>Other Web Sites for Career Path Research</u> After discovering some interesting career paths in the *Occupational Outlook Handbook,* you need to explore those paths further by looking at other career Web sites, of which there are literally hundreds. You can find a wealth of information on any type of career you can imagine by searching the Web sites of professional associations, colleges and universities, and job banks, as well as general career search engines such as www.monster.com and www.hotjobs.com. And, don't forget to go to the related sites you found in the *Occupational Outlook Handbook.* Consult as many Web sites as you have time for, obtaining descriptions of career paths and the jobs within them.

Here is a list of Web sites to help you explore the accounting profession:

http://community.hotjobs.com/hj-accounting

http://accounting.smartpros.com/x29668.xml

http://www.quintcareers.com/career_exploration.html

http://www.acinet.org/acinet/explore.htm

http://www.vaultreports.com/hubs/501/channelhome_501.jsp?ch_id=253

Recommendation for Action Go on-line and find five Web sites relevant to the field in which you are interested. Record the URLs and all useful items of information from each site below:

URL	Information

Business, Professional, and Trade Publications Once you have some background information, business and professional publications can bring you up-to-date and clarify what it's like to work in the business world and, more specifically, in the accounting profession.

For your general business knowledge, read daily and weekly publications, such as the business section of your local newspaper, *The Wall Street Journal,* and *Business Week.* These publications should be available in print at your school or public library, in your school or public library's periodicals database, or by discounted subscription through your school's accounting, finance, or business department.

Articles in professional publications are an excellent way to discover current information about the accounting profession because they focus on breaking news, developing trends, changes in the industry, and predictions for the future. *The Journal of Accountancy* and *The Practicing Accountant,* both available on the Web site of the American Institute of CPAs (www.aicpa.org), provide current practice information for public accountants. *Strategic Accountant,* published by the Institute of Management Accountants, contains the latest in developments in corporate accounting and finance (www.strategicfinancemag.com).

An excellent publication that is specifically geared to college accounting students is *New Accountant,* published every other month and available either in print or on-line by bulk subscription to your school or by individual subscription. *New Accountant* publishes information that is highly relevant to college students on accounting careers, job searching, and workplace and technology issues. If your school does not subscribe, ask one of your accounting professors to consider it. *New Accountant's* Web address is www.newaccountantUSA.com.

Recommendation for Action Go to your school or public library and consult the periodicals database. Find the latest edition of *The Wall Street Journal* or *Business Week* and peruse it from cover to cover. Find at least two articles on subjects that interest you and read them in their entirety. Make note of the articles in the space below. Next, find on-line the latest edition of the *Journal of Accountancy, The Practicing CPA,* or *Strategic Accountant.* Find at least two articles on subjects that interest you and read them in their entirety, making note of them in the space below. Finally, make a plan to continue your business reading as often as you can—if not daily, then at least on a weekly basis.

Publication	Date	Article	Notes

Informational Interviewing Although information from the Web and printed sources is ideal for providing background, the best way to get a feel for a job is to talk with people about it. Informational interviewing is a technique that helps you to identify people with whom to discuss potential jobs and to structure conversations that will enlarge your understanding. Informational interviewing is an indispensable step in the career search, not only because it helps you refine your knowledge of the field you're exploring but also because it helps you develop the social skills you need to succeed in employment interviews.

Begin the process of informational interviewing by identifying contacts working in the job that interests you. Brainstorm lists of names of:

- relatives
- friends
- friends of your parents
- teachers
- former employers
- neighbors
- church members

Now, narrow your list to four or five people who are involved with the career paths you found interesting during your Web research. Then, get ready to call each person on your "short list."

To get ready, you must first overcome any reluctance you have about calling strangers or people whom you know only slightly. If you feel hesitant or shy, just remember that most people really like to talk about themselves and will be happy to do so with you!

Next, think about what information you're seeking and prepare questions that will help you obtain it. The suggestions that follow will help you get started, but be sure to draft specific questions of your own.

You should plan to conduct several phone interviews and at least one on-site interview. You'll learn much more by interviewing someone in his or her workplace than you will by talking on the phone. Why? You'll have the benefit of face-to-face contact, which will allow you to read nonverbal as well as verbal signals. You will also be able to observe the workplace firsthand, to get a feel for the pace of the job, to see how people interact with one another, and so forth.

Questions for Informational Interviews Because you are doing preliminary research, you should plan to ask "open" questions rather than "closed" ones. Open questions get people talking. They offer respondents the chance to give both broad and in-depth answers. Open questions often begin with the words *how, what, why,* and *where.* Closed questions narrow the focus of the interview. Closed questions force respondents to choose among two or more possible answers (*yes* or *no; method a, b,* or *c*). Questions that ask for specific information (names, dates, etc.) are closed. Closed questions often begin with such words as *do you/did you, when, who,* and *how many.*

Here are some sample questions to get you started. You will want to develop more on your own. Others will occur to you as you're doing the interview.

1. What is your organization in business to do?
2. Does your organization make products? Provide services? Can you tell me about them?
3. What are some similar organizations in the industry?
4. When your company hires recent college graduates, what kinds of jobs do they get?
5. What qualifications do entry-level college graduates need?
6. What kinds of positions are available for student accounting majors? Summer jobs? Internships? Externships?
7. How does a person move up in your company? Are there lots of opportunities for advancement?

8. What kind of training do new people go through?
9. What advice would you give a college accounting major who wanted to get into this line of work?

If you feel you've established a good rapport with your interviewee, or if he or she is someone you know fairly well, you might move on to more specific questions:

10. What's a "day in the life" on your job like?
11. What's the best thing about your job?
12. What's the worst thing about your job?
13. How does your job fit into the "big picture" of the organization?
14. How did you get into this kind of work?
15. What would you say about salaries for entry-level people on this job?
16. What's the working environment like at your job? Laid-back? Formal? High-pressure? Stressful? Competitive?
17. What kinds of people do really well in this job? What kinds of skills are needed to make it to the top?
18. What related occupations would you suggest that someone investigate?
19. Could you give me the names of other people in this field whom I might speak with?

Recommendations for Action

1. Make an appointment with one or more of your professors, a campus career counselor, a friend or family member, or other connection who can give you general advice about the business world or advice about one of your career paths of interest. Arrange to telephone or to go and meet with those individuals to conduct informational interviews.
2. Before conducting your interviews, prepare a list of questions you'd like to ask. During the interview, take notes. Ask for clarification if necessary. At the end of your interviews, be sure to ask for names of other people in your field of interest whom you might be able to interview.
3. After the interview, summarize the information you've obtained and save it.

Internships To deepen your exploration of the accounting profession, you should seek internships relevant to the career path(s) you're interested in during your sophomore and junior summers and during your junior and senior school years. If you spend your freshman and sophomore years exploring the profession and preparing a résumé, you will be ready to apply for internships during the spring of your sophomore year. As you add each internship to your résumé, you will be able to list valuable experience and skills relevant to your eventual job search.

Internships are part-time jobs—sometimes paid, sometimes unpaid, sometimes for college credit, sometimes not—and are available through your college or university. They represent your best opportunity to gain experience relevant to your future career while you are in school. These programs give you the chance to meet working professionals who can help you later in your job search. They also give you contacts at firms and companies where you may later want to work.

If you are interested in doing an internship (and every accounting major should be), your first point of contact will probably be with your school's placement office. There, you can find out what kind of internships are available in your area of interest, names of companies offering

Figure 2—Interviewing for an Internship

internships and when, and whether or not the positions are paid. Let your career placement counselor know that you'd like to sign up for an internship, and he or she will explain the application/registration procedure to you and probably ask you to provide a résumé (see the following sections).

You should expect to have to interview for an internship position, just as you would for a full-time job, so you'll want to learn about interviewing and what to wear (see the later sections on interviewing and business attire).

Once you begin working at your internship, you will see first-hand what an accounting workplace is like and what it's like to do the actual work involved. You will have a work site supervisor to report to, and that supervisor will evaluate your work and your progress to your internship advisor on campus. By the end of your internship, you will have gained experience and gathered information that may help you decide whether or not that type of accounting career would be right for you.

REMEMBER: Every office environment is as different as the people who work there. Even if you are not thrilled with a particular internship experience, a similar job in a different office culture might turn out to be right for you.

Recommendation for Action Consult the Web site, http://accounting.smartpros.com/x14382.xml, which provides an excellent collection of general information about internships. Then, visit your school's placement office and browse through its listings of internships in various accounting and finance fields. Ask for a copy of the application procedures required and familiarize yourself with them. Make an appointment to meet with a placement counselor to discuss your plans for doing an internship.

Now that you've explored some accounting career paths that interest you, it's time to start looking for just the right job with the right company or firm.

RESEARCHING THE JOB MARKET

How Do I Find the Job That I Want?

As an accounting student, you have many sources of job information. Investigate each one thoroughly.

College Placement Office   The placement office at your college or university is a rich source of information on employment trends and jobs. Most placement offices maintain libraries with reference materials on local, national, and international career opportunities, salary scales in various industries, guidelines for writing résumés and cover letters, tips for effective interviewing, and other topics. Many employers send announcements of job openings to college placement offices; some arrange recruiting efforts through these offices as well. At large institutions, the business school or accounting department may have a separate placement office.

Get to know your placement director and counselors. Ask them for advice on researching the job market. Make an appointment to have them review your résumé. Schedule time for mock job interviews. Colleges pay placement counselors to help you launch your career. Take advantage of this free service.

Job Fairs   Many universities and local chapters of professional accounting associations, such as state CPA institutes, the Institute of Management Accountants (IMA), the Institute of Internal Auditors (IIA), and others, sponsor job fairs to help students find employment. These fairs are one- or two-day events that bring in recruiters from large corporations, accounting firms, banks, nonprofit organizations, government agencies, and other places to advertise available jobs and to recruit students. In large urban areas, job fairs often draw hundreds of recruiters. Smaller colleges and chapters of accounting associations occasionally sponsor job fairs with one another to draw large numbers as well.

Job fairs give you the chance to talk informally with potential employers, to present your résumé for possible openings, and to learn more about specific companies. A job fair may be your first contact with your employer-to-be. If you plan to attend one of these events, dress in business attire, bring a number of résumés, and be prepared to ask intelligent questions about the employer and to answer questions about yourself. For on-line help in locating career fairs in your area, consult http://careerfairs.com.

Your Professors   Professors of accounting often have wide networks of contacts. Many professors had successful careers as accountants themselves before they turned to teaching, and they remain in close touch with former colleagues. Others, who have gone straight from Ph.D. programs to the classroom, are active in professional associations such as the AICPA and in state and local CPA societies and institutes, where they work on committees with practitioners. Make appointments with several of your professors and interview them about possible contacts at the firms or companies that interest you.

The World Wide Web   Most large employers now use the Web to recruit applicants, posting job openings through their own sites or job advertisements on commercial employment sites.

These Web sites not only provide information on employment opportunities but also allow applicants to submit résumés on-line.

General Searches If you are just beginning your job search, or if you want a broad overview of opportunities in accounting, general search engines such as Yahoo!, Google, and others are excellent sources of information. Each of these engines has a jobs or careers category, which links to one of many commercial employment sites on the Web. Employers pay the costs associated with advertising and recruiting through these sites, which are an excellent source of information about openings in various accounting specialties and geographical locations. Some sites, such as www.nationjob.com and www.monster.com, offer job seekers e-mail notification options, collecting information on all jobs that match an applicant's search criteria and sending announcements of those jobs to the applicant's e-mail address. Remember, however, that each employment site you consult has different employer subscribers. To get a broad overview of opportunities, visit as many sites as possible.

Some Web sites are dedicated specifically to the accounting and finance job markets. Check out www.accounting.com, www.inthemoney.com, and www.financialjobs.com for direct access to jobs in your fields of interest. Some sites will ask you to "sign in" with résumé information, but don't worry. These sites are free to job seekers.

Here is a list of some other helpful job search Web sites:

www.hotjobs.com/htdocs/channels/accounting/

www.collegegrad.com/jobsearch/index.shtml

www.quintcareers.com/researching_companies.html

www.careerweb.com/jobs/

www.vaultreports.com/jobs/jobboard/searchform.jsp

www.brassring.com/cim/cim_employersearch.asp

Web Sites of Accounting Firms If you have a more specific idea of the jobs you are seeking, you can find information through firm and company Web sites. For job openings in public accounting, use the Rutgers University accounting gateway at http://www.rutgers.edu/Accounting. This megasite is a clearinghouse for much of the accounting information on the Web. It offers links to the Web sites of the country's largest multinational public firms, such as PricewaterhouseCoopers and Ernst & Young, each of which recruits new employees electronically, and to sites of hundreds of other public accounting firms, many of which post job opportunities as well. These Web sites offer job seekers valuable help, explaining what qualities the firms are looking for in job applicants, offering advice on preparing résumés and providing templates for submitting them, and giving tips on preparing for interviews.

A list of the top 100 accounting firms in the United States can be found at http://accounting.smartpros.com/x5168.xml#Top100.

Web Sites of Companies For jobs in private accounting, Web search engines can help you locate job openings quickly and easily. If you know you want to work for a certain company, go directly to that company's Web site and follow the career links to job postings. If the company you're interested in doesn't post job openings on its Web site, use the site to find out the company's phone number and/or mailing address, and contact people directly for application information.

Recommendation for Action Go to www.accounting.com or another Web site of your choosing and identify at least five employers offering internships or jobs in your chosen career path(s). Record company names, phone numbers, Web addresses, contact persons (if available), and job titles of interest:

1. Company:______________________________Web:______________________
   Phone:______________________Contact:___________________________
   Job Titles____
2. Company:______________________________Web:______________________
   Phone:______________________Contact:___________________________
   Job Titles____
3. Company:______________________________Web:______________________
   Phone:______________________Contact:___________________________
   Job Titles____
4. Company:______________________________Web:______________________
   Phone:______________________Contact:___________________________
   Job Titles____
5. Company:______________________________Web:______________________
   Phone:______________________Contact:___________________________
   Job Titles____

Plan to send your résumé and cover letter to each of the companies you've identified to ask for an interview for an internship or a job. To get your résumé and cover letters ready for the job market, follow the advice given in the next section.

PREPARING A RÉSUMÉ

What Is the Purpose of a Résumé?

Many people assume that a résumé is a summary of qualifications that should lead to a job offer. Wrong! A résumé is a *sales instrument* designed to get you an interview. A good résumé sells the employer on the idea that you are worth talking to. Your communication skills, poise, interviewing savvy, knowledge, and experience do the rest.

Because a résumé is a sales tool targeted to a specific employer, it must be very carefully tailored to that employer's needs. Do not assume that you can "do a résumé" and use it for any and all jobs you are seeking. Your résumé changes over time, and it should change from job application to job application. Although you can prepare a master draft, you may need to re-tool the résumé every time you apply for an internship or a job so that you can shape the information to fit that individual job.

What Type of Résumé Do I Need?

Résumés fall into three basic categories: the *chronological résumé,* the *functional résumé,* and the *combination résumé.*

The chronological résumé presents qualifications in reverse chronological order, emphasizing positions held, degrees obtained, and dates. The functional résumé presents qualifications in terms of the skills the applicant can bring to the job, with less emphasis on the sequence of work experience. The combination type emphasizes functional skills at the beginning and lists career-related experience in reverse chronological order at the end.

While the chronological approach can be very effective for people with a substantial career track record, the ***functional approach is the best choice*** for those still new to the job market—undergraduates and graduating seniors.

When Do I Need My First Résumé?

Because you'll be seeking summer jobs and internships as an undergraduate accounting major, you need to have a résumé ready as early as your sophomore year. Because you are new to the job market, your qualifications will be based more on personal characteristics and transferable skills than on work experience. The guidelines that follow will help you prepare a functional résumé that emphasizes your transferable skills. Use it to apply for positions related to your major throughout your undergraduate years. As you acquire accounting-specific skills and experience through internships, jobs, and volunteer work, add this information to your résumé. By your senior year, your functional résumé will have grown to a combination type—one that presents both skills and experience in the best possible light.

How Do I Begin?

<u>Assess Your Talents and Strengths</u> Because you need to prepare a functional résumé, assessing your qualifications is more complicated than simply listing your educational credentials and work experience. It involves thinking about your talents and strengths, identifying what you are especially good at, and recognizing where you have been particularly effective in projects and interpersonal situations. Then, it involves thinking about how these talents and strengths "translate" into the skills and traits employers seek in those they hire:

- Strong work ethic
- Dependability and maturity
- Flexibility and creative thinking
- Leadership
- Team spirit
- "Grace under pressure"
- Communication skills
- Computer skills
- Technical knowledge

Brainstorm for a few minutes about your strengths and talents. Divide a piece of paper into two columns. At the top of the left column, write "Strengths, talents." You will come up with all manner of things: working math problems, convincing people to buy things, helping friends with their homework, finding mistakes in other people's work, using the computer, and so on. List each of these things on a separate line. Don't censor yourself! Write down everything.

When you've listed a lot of things you're good at, create another heading in the left column, below your last entry: "Activities and jobs." List extracurricular activities, volunteer work, sorority/fraternity activities, community and civic work, church activities, internships, paid employment, and so forth.

Identify Transferable Skills Now that you've listed your strengths as well as your experience, it is time to analyze how these translate into the kinds of traits and skills employers value. Go back to the top of the page, this time to the right column. On the first line, write "Trait, characteristic, or transferable skill." Review each entry you have made in the left column; explain in the right column how each item offers evidence of an important workplace skill. If you have noted, for example, that you're good at finding mistakes in your fellow students' homework, translate that strength into a skill that's valuable in accounting: "Excellent attention to detail and accuracy."

Repeat this process for the activities and jobs in the lower part of the left column. If you were president of your high school sorority, translate that experience into "Leadership ability and strong interpersonal skills." If you tutored other students in math during college, translate that work into "Technical knowledge and communication skills."

The résumé self-assessment worksheet shown in Figure 3 gives you a model for this process.

Emily Baskin
Résumé Self-Assessment Worksheet

Strengths, talents	Trait, characteristic, or transferable skill
Projects (not tests)	Organized, good at initiating work, coming up with ideas and ways to solve problems, bringing projects to completion
Classroom oral presentations	Oral communication skills, writing skills, computer skills (Power Point)
Numbers, math	Technical ability with accounting techniques
Excel spreadsheets	Computer skills (Excel)
Getting the numbers to work out	Math ability, perseverance, concentration
Getting things done on time	Punctuality, ability to meet deadlines
Handling lots of things at the same time (multiple assignments, tutoring, my internship)	Multi-tasking abilities; organized, good time management, energy, work ethic
Getting people to work well together (team projects, summer job, my roommates in the dorm)	Friendly, diplomatic, communication skills (listening), team working, leadership
Learning new software packages	Computer skills (tax software and CCH service, accounting packages)
Selling to customers (Christmas job)	Customer relations, communication skills, enthusiasm
Explaining accounting when I tutor (well, the students say so)	Ability to communicate, to teach; patience, evidence of accounting knowledge
Activities and jobs	
High school tennis team	Leadership, team spirit, energetic
High school newspaper staff writer	Written communication skills
Big Sky Accounting and Finance Club	Commitment to school, interest in accounting
Big Sky varsity tennis	Leadership, team spirit, energetic, time management
Christmas job at Bath & Body Works	Sales, organization (organized stock of products)
Tutoring at Big Sky: Financial, Managerial, Tax, Intermediate I and II	Oral communication (see above)
VITA tax assistance program, junior and senior spring terms	Tax and tax software knowledge, community involvement, customer relations, communication skills, time management
Henley Brothers job	Knowledge of cash account management, accounts receivable and payable, dealing with customers, financial statement preparation, supervising employees, training of new employees (communication, technical knowledge), responsibility
Internship with Bill Sinclair's CPA firm	Technical knowledge: Excel used, accounting software learned, tax software learned, CCH on-line tax service used, tax return preparation: federal, state, and local for individuals, partnerships, corporations (small business), payroll tax return preparation, monthly statement preparation for small business clients

Figure 3—Sample Résumé Self-Assessment Worksheet

Recommendation for Action Prepare your own résumé self-assessment worksheet in a word processing file or on the blank worksheet provided here.

Name:
Résumé Self-Assessment Worksheet

Strengths, talents	**Trait, characteristic, or transferable skill**
Activities and jobs	

How Do I Put My Résumé Together?

To do its job (getting your foot in the door), your résumé has to grab attention *fast*. According to career professionals, readers make their *yes* or *no* decisions on résumés within 10 to 20 seconds. Therefore, the first things they see—on the top half of the résumé—are the most important elements. To organize your résumé for maximum impact, include the following components in this order:

1. heading
2. career objective statement
3. summary of qualifications
4. summary of technical skills
5. section on education
6. section on experience
7. section on activities, if applicable

Emily's sample résumé (Figure 4) illustrates these components.

Emily A. Baskin
baskine@bigsky.edu

Home: 8412 Oak Hollow Drive
Eden, WY 82926
(823) 946-5555

Campus: 1 University Drive
Casper, WY 82001
(809) 611-4444

Objective
To obtain a position with a regional public accounting firm where strong communication and technical skills are essential to the firm's development.

Summary of Qualifications
- A *successful communicator* with excellent *interpersonal and team skills* developed through interaction at school and work and through Big Sky's communication-intensive accounting curriculum
- A *quick, detail-oriented learner* and *creative problem solver,* proven through interning with William Sinclair, CPA, and through experience in corporate accounting at Henley Brothers
- An *effective time manager and multi-tasker,* highly *motivated to succeed,* evidenced by achieving a strong GPA while peer tutoring, volunteering, and playing varsity tennis

Technical Skills
- Proficiency in Microsoft Excel, Word, and Power Point; Internet research and e-mail
- Tax return preparation, both manual and computerized using Turbo Tax
- Basic tax law research using CCH on-line tax service
- Financial statement preparation and recordkeeping for small business

Education
Big Sky University, B.S. in Accounting, May 2002. Overall GPA 3.5 / Accounting GPA 3.7

Experience
Fall 2001 — William Sinclair, CPA — Casper, WY
Public Accounting Internship
- Prepared tax returns for corporate, partnership, and individual clients
- Maintained books, prepared payroll taxes, and compiled monthly financial statements

Summers 1999–2001 — Henley Brothers, Inc. — Casper, WY
Corporate Accounting / Money Management
- Managed cash receipts and reconciled bank and customer accounts
- Supervised and trained employees at corporate and divisional offices

Spring 2001 and 2002 — IRS VITA-TCE Program — Casper, WY
Student Volunteer Income Tax Return Preparation

2000–2002 — Big Sky University — Casper, WY
Student Peer Tutoring—Accounting Curriculum

December 2000 and 2001 — Bath & Body Works, Inc. — Eden, WY
Sales / Stock Management

Activities
- Member, Big Sky Accounting and Finance Club
- Team Captain, Big Sky University Varsity Tennis

Figure 4—Sample Résumé

Think of your résumé in two parts—the first section, where you "advertise yourself" and grab the reader's attention, and the second section, where you provide evidence of what you've asserted above. The first section, which includes *the heading, the career objective statement, the summary of qualifications,* and *the summary of technical skills,* describes your abilities, talents, and achievements. The second section, which includes *education and experience,* establishes your educational credentials and work history.

<u>Heading</u> Begin with a heading containing your personal information. This section, positioned at the top of the résumé, lets employers know how to get in touch with you, so it's essential that the information be accurate and up-to-date. It lists your name (first, middle initial, last), your address(es) (home and campus, if different), and your phone number(s). Include your e-mail address and plan to check your e-mail regularly. ***Never put the word "résumé" in your heading.***

Recommendation for Action Open a new word-processing file in which you will write your résumé. Prepare your heading according to the guidelines you've just read. Then, create headings for each of the other six components of a functional format résumé.

<u>Career Objective Statement</u> The career objective statement tells prospective employers that you know exactly what you want to do. Vague and general objective statements do more harm than good. If you say you're seeking "an interesting position in the accounting field," your résumé is destined for the wastebasket. Therefore, before you begin, decide on a specific job title toward which to direct your objective. Remember: You may have to revise parts of your résumé for each job application. The career objective statement is one element you will revise over and over.

A good career objective statement not only shows that you know what you're looking for but also tells the employer what you can bring to the job. Although the statement should define the job you seek, it should be grounded in an understanding of what the employer will be looking for in the person to be hired. To craft an effective objective statement, ask yourself:

What is this employer looking for in an entry-level candidate/intern for this position?

What skills and abilities are especially important for this job?

What characteristics will make me stand out?

And don't just ask yourself; ask others, too. Talk to people in the field to find answers to these questions. If you know someone working in the firm or company you're applying to, seek answers there. Give yourself as clear a picture as you can of the successful candidate for this job. Then, present yourself as that candidate in your career objective statement.

Example: You're applying for an entry-level position with a local public accounting firm.

Ineffective objective: To obtain an entry-level staff position in a small public accounting firm with plans to grow.

To revise, try using this formula: a [type of, name of] position in a [firm, company] where [relevant skill] and [relevant skill] would/could [be needed, contribute to company's need].

Better: To obtain a staff position in a local public accounting firm where excellent communication skills and strong computer knowledge can contribute to the organization's growth.

The revised objective shows that the writer has thought about the qualities that will make him stand out. Instead of saying, "Here's what *I* want in a job," it says "I have the skills to make a difference in *your* firm."

Recommendation for Action With a specific internship or job in mind, write an objective statement that names the position you're seeking and describes the skills that you can bring to the job. Enter this statement into your résumé.

Summary of Qualifications This section gives you the chance to focus your reader's attention on the personal characteristics and transferable skills that will make you successful on the job. It's a particularly important part of the résumé of college students, whose work experience is necessarily limited.

Because space is also limited, the summary should consist of several brief phrases in which every word counts. These phrases should emphasize strengths *(well-organized, fast learner)* and skills *(time management, problem-solving).*

Go back to your self-assessment worksheet. Take the most relevant traits and skills from the right column and combine them as positively as you can.

Note how our sample student, Emily Baskin, has phrased these statements on her résumé (see Figure 4). She describes herself as "a *successful communicator* with excellent *interpersonal and team skills," a "quick, detail-oriented learner* and *creative problem solver,"* and an *"effective time manager and multi-tasker, highly motivated to succeed."*

Recommendation for Action Refer to your self-assessment worksheet and choose five or six of your strongest transferable skills. Be sure to consider whether those skills would be of value to the firm to which you're applying. Construct three statements for your summary of qualifications, following the guidelines described above and using Emily's résumé as a model. Add these statements to your résumé.

Summary of Technical Skills This section is particularly important for accounting students because of the specialized knowledge the career requires. It should include:

- A list of software mastered
- A list of any unusual or unique accounting coursework or relevant coursework outside your major
- A list of skills relevant to accounting practice, acquired through coursework, class projects, internships, volunteer work, and/or jobs

You may also want to include:

- A list of skills which are not "technical" per se, such as sales ability, oral presentation skills, and interpersonal skills if you deem these skills an asset to the job for which you are applying with this résumé.

Recommendation for Action Describe your technical skills under your heading of summary of technical skills.

The second half of your résumé provides evidence to back up the assertions you've made about your qualifications in section one. This evidence takes the form of your educational background and work history.

<u>Education</u> This section establishes your educational credentials. If you have distinguished yourself in any way during college (Dean's List, academic honors, awards), include that information here. List:

- the college you attended or are attending and its location, unless the name makes that clear (if you have attended more than one college, include only the school from which you received or will receive your degree)
- any study abroad programs you have attended
- any graduate study (even if you did not complete a degree)
- the degree(s) you earned or will earn
- the date or expected date of your graduation
- information on progress toward the 150-hour requirement (if required by the state in which you are applying)

Do not include high school information.

Also list:

- your major(s) and minor(s)
- your grade-point averages (overall and in your major, if it's higher) if over 3.0
- any special recognitions, awards, or achievements (Dean's List, exceptional class rank, graduation with honors, special awards)

In the sample résumé, Emily notes that she is graduating in May 2002, that her overall GPA is 3.5, and that her GPA in her major is 3.7.

Recommendation for Action Under your education heading, describe your educational credentials following the guidelines given above. Be as complete as possible.

<u>Experience</u> This section gives employers evidence, at a glance, of your qualifications and skills.

List all relevant experience in reverse chronological order (starting with the most recent experience and working backward). Include:

- place of work/name of firm or company
- city and state
- job title
- dates of work
- brief description of duties

For graduating seniors, the scope and variety of your experience will demonstrate the effort you put into career preparation while you were in school. A résumé with relevant summer work, internships, volunteer experience, and relevant positions in service organizations creates a picture of a person with initiative and motivation to get ahead. Be sure to list non-accounting experience in this section as well, as your non-accounting jobs will have helped provide the transferable skills you've listed in the first section.

A good approach to preparing the experience section of your résumé is to make a list of all the tasks you performed on each job, then choose those two or three tasks that give the clearest possible idea of the nature of the work you did.

Be specific and don't be afraid to toot your own horn. If you handled large amounts of money on a job or worked for several people, list the numbers. Specific numbers help your reader visualize the workload. If your job performance was recognized as outstanding, make a note of that as well. In fact, if you made special contributions to any organization or distinguished yourself in any way, be sure to say so and explain in detail.

Don't allow the tasks you performed to sound mundane. Instead of saying "worked in the controller's office doing accounts receivable, clerical tasks, and bank reconciliations," say "designed Excel spreadsheets for analysis of customer accounts, assisted controller's team in quarterly budget preparation, reconciled monthly bank statements to company books."

If you were assistant manager at TGIFridays, say, "supervised a wait staff of seven; was responsible for daily cash deposits of $3,000–$6,000, dealt with customers and handled complaints." By describing your experience in this way, you show potential employers not only what you did but also what you learned on the job.

Recommendation for Action Under your experience heading, describe the internships and/or jobs you've had as well as any volunteer work you've done. Keep your descriptions of duties brief, but be specific and show what you learned.

Congratulations! You've just finished a first draft of your résumé.

What Should My Résumé Look Like?

When you've finished a draft of your résumé, you may need to revise to fit all of your information on one page or to format your material for easy reading. Remember: Career professionals almost unanimously advise that entry-level job seekers limit résumés to a single page. If you have a lot of information, choose a compact font such as Times or Times New Roman. If your résumé is a bit sketchy, choose a larger font such as Palatino or New Century Schoolbook. You can get away with 11-point type rather than the standard 12-point if you need to shrink your résumé a bit, but any font smaller than 11-point will be hard to read and is not recommended. (Emily's résumé was reduced to fit on its page.) Another way to adapt your material effectively to the one-page requirement is to make use of the full width of the page to lay out your material.

Your résumé should be laser printed on 100% rag bond, white or ivory only. It should be error free.

What Should I Do to Finish?

When you have revised your résumé to your satisfaction, proofread it diligently, ask others to proofread it, and edit to correct all errors. Typos and grammar errors in a résumé are a sign of carelessness and suggest that any other work you produce might be careless as well. Check your grammar: Your descriptions of experience should consistently use the simple past tense of the verb (*performed, provided*) unless you are listing present or continuing employment. In that case, you should use the present tense. If you have separated items with commas or semi-colons in your summary of qualifications or skills, make sure your use is consistent. Make sure you have used proper postal codes for the names of any states you have abbreviated, and check the phone numbers you have listed for transposed numbers or other errors.

Recommendation for Action Review your résumé and revise for spelling and grammar, check for consistent use of punctuation marks and for attractive fonts, and assess whether your layout is easy to follow.

Now show your résumé to several people who can give you constructive criticism: placement personnel, professors, parents, and business people you know. Consider making changes to your résumé based on what your reviewers have said.

Where Do I List My References?

Do not list references on your résumé. Do not even say "references available upon request." Your reader knows you will provide references, and saying so only wastes space. After you're satisfied with your résumé, prepare a separate reference sheet that you can send to a prospective employer upon request. The reference sheet lists those people who know your work and are willing to answer inquiries about you.

Listings should include names of your references with their titles, their organizations, their addresses, their e-mail addresses, and current office phone numbers. Be sure to ask all references for permission to use their names before including them on your list. Contact them by phone, e-mail, or formal letter to explain what jobs you are seeking and what help you are requesting. Only place their names on the list after you have received permission.

Also, send each person on your list a copy of your résumé and application letters so that he or she will know what you are emphasizing about yourself to prospective employers. If you think additional materials (copies of class papers or projects, projects at work, etc.) will help anyone on your list remember you more clearly and speak more highly of you, send these materials as well.

Plan to take a copy of your résumé and your reference sheet to the job interview. Emily's reference sheet follows (Figure 5).

References

Emily A. Baskin
1 University Drive
Casper, WY 82001
(809) 611-4444
baskine@bigsky.edu

Mr. William Sinclair, CPA
7482 Lone Pine Street
Casper, WY 82001
(809) 573-8923
wsinclcpa@aol.com

Dr. Margaret Langston
Professor of Accounting
Big Sky University
Department of Accounting
P.O. Box 65574
Casper, WY 82001
(809) 611-3790
Langston@bsu.edu

Ms. Janet Stewart
Assistant Controller
Henley Brothers, Inc.
980 Roosevelt Street
Eden, WY 82926
(809) 376-8024
jstewrt@henleybros.com

Dr. Brian Foreman
Associate Professor of Accounting
Big Sky University
Department of Accounting
P.O. Box 65574
Casper, WY 82001
(809) 611-3790
bforeman@bsu.edu

Figure 5—Sample Reference Sheet

Recommendation for Action Identify three or four people who might offer you references. Ideally, your reference list should include people with whom you have studied and people for whom you have worked, so that employers can get a well-rounded picture of you by talking with each of them. Jot down several names.

Next, think about which of these people will give you the strongest recommendation. One of your professors? An internship supervisor? An employer? Put that person's name at the top of your list. The second strongest? Place that name next, and so forth.

Contact all the people you plan to include on your reference sheet (by phone, by e-mail, or by letter). Ask permission to include them, remind them about your work in class or on the job, and tell them that prospective employers may be calling. Also, send each person on your list a copy of your résumé and application letters.

After obtaining permission from your references and sending your materials, prepare your list of references by following Emily's model.

WRITING COVER LETTERS

Always send your résumé with a cover letter that highlights your unique qualifications for the job.

Cover letters should be brief and follow standard formats for professional correspondence. They should be printed on the same 100% rag bond as your résumé. The guidelines in the next section will help you draft cover letters that do the job well.

How Do I Get Started?

Prepare to write your cover letter by gathering information about the position and about the firm or company to which you are applying. Always make every effort to determine who is in charge of hiring at the firm or company, and address your cover letter to that person by name and title. If you cannot find out the individual's name, use the appropriate title ("Dear Human Resources Director") or address the letter to the appropriate committee ("Dear Personnel Committee"). Do not write "To Whom It May Concern" salutations.

Cover letters should not rehash your résumé. Instead, they should achieve these three purposes (plan to devote a paragraph to each one):

1. Identify whether your application is solicited or unsolicited
2. Explain how your qualifications fit the position for which you are applying
3. Ask for an interview

<u>Paragraph 1: Solicited vs. Unsolicited Applications</u> When employers open application letters, the first thing they want to know is whether you're responding to a solicitation they've made for applicants or writing to inquire about job possibilities.

As we noted earlier, most employers solicit applications for entry-level jobs through word-of-mouth, position announcements in newspapers, and job postings on university campuses. Many firms and corporations also recruit entry-level applicants at job fairs and recruiting sessions on campuses. Still others, invite applications through their home pages on the World Wide Web.

Explaining the reason for your application helps orient your reader. Along with the career objective statement on your résumé, this explanation helps your reader categorize your inquiry. The first paragraph of your cover letter should indicate the position for which you are applying and where you learned of the position (if solicited).

Example:

Dear Ms. Walshok:

Please consider my application for one of the entry-level staff positions your firm recently advertised at the Central Valley Job Fair.

If someone with whom the reader is acquainted (a professor, a colleague, or a business connection) has suggested that you apply, be sure to say so in the first or second sentence. If you have had an internship at the firm or company and have been invited to apply for a full-time position, make this fact clear in the first paragraph as well.

Example:

Dear Mr. Villani:

Please accept this application for the position of staff accountant at Texas Instruments. After my summer internship in the controller's office last year, Ms. Janet Stewart, assistant controller, suggested I seek full-time employment with the company.

If your application is unsolicited, explain that you are interested in a position should one be available:

Example:

Dear Mr. Honeywell:

I am writing to apply for an entry-level audit position with your firm, should such an opening exist.

Paragraph 2: Your Qualifications for the Position The body of the cover letter should show the reader what you can bring to the job that will make you an asset to the organization. You've made that point on your résumé, but the reader hasn't seen your résumé yet. So, take this opportunity to put your best foot forward, too. Don't just rehash the information on your résumé, however. Use the cover letter to draw attention to the highlights of your résumé:

Ineffective: I worked as an accounting intern last summer at Del Rios Engineering in Madrid, Spain.

Better: My internship at Del Rios Engineering in Madrid, Spain, gave me valuable experience in cross-cultural business practices as well as a grounding in international corporate accounting.

The ineffective example merely repeats a fact from the résumé, but the revised sentence highlights the job applicant's technical knowledge.

To draft the body of the cover letter, review your self-assessment worksheet. Choose the two or three items that best exemplify those qualities you want to emphasize and condense each entry into a sentence or two. Emily's worksheet might yield the following paragraphs:

Example:

At Big Sky University, I maintained a 3.7 GPA in accounting while working as a volunteer tax preparer and student tutor for 25 hours per week. This record illustrates my commitment to the work ethic, my determination to achieve my goals, and my ability to handle multiple tasks effectively.

My strong academic performance also attests to my professional communication skills; the accounting program at Big Sky is communications-intensive throughout the curriculum. I was able to build on this academic foundation with a summer internship and job that gave me valuable practical experience in public and corporate accounting.

These sentences will form the backbone of your second paragraph.

Paragraph 3: Asking for an Interview Conclude your cover letter by politely asking for an interview and explaining how you can be reached to set one up. Although you have listed your address(es), phone number(s), and your e-mail address on your résumé, use your cover letter to explain any unusual circumstances or details the reader may need in order to contact you. If you are applying for a job in another city, for example, and plan to be there on a certain date, your cover letter should communicate that information. If you are frequently away from your phone and want prospective employers to leave voice mail messages for you, say so. Do not forget, of course, to close with your thanks.

Example: I will be in the Chicago area during the week of June 10 and would welcome the chance to talk with you about the position at that time. If you would like to arrange an interview, please call me at (209) 432-8967. Thank you for your consideration.

Example: I would like to present my qualifications to you in person. I will call you in a week or two to see if an interview is possible. In the meantime, I can be reached at (254) 756-3901. Thank you for considering my application.

How Do I Put the Letter Together?

Assemble the elements you have generated thus far, adding transitions and details as necessary. Format your letter using the standard elements of business correspondence:

1. Heading (your address with city, state, and zip code, and the date)
2. Inside address (name, title, organization, and full address of recipient)
3. Salutation (traditional greeting, followed by a colon)
4. Body (letter content)
5. Complimentary close (courtesy phrase: sincerely, yours truly, etc.)
6. Signature (sign above your typed full name)
7. Enclosure line (indicates that résumé or other materials accompany letter)

Choose either full block style (in which every line begins flush with the left margin) or modified block style (in which the heading, complimentary close, and signature are aligned immediately to the right of center and everything else is aligned flush with the left margin). Full block style is more formal and is the predominant choice for workplace correspondence. Modified block is "friendlier"; you might want to use it if you are writing to someone with whom you are already acquainted via an internship or other professional connections.

Emily A. Baskin
1 University Drive
Casper, WY 82001

Heading

March 11, 2002

Hunter V. Layton
Human Resources Director
Henley Brothers, Inc.
980 Roosevelt Street
Eden, WY 82926

Inside Address

Dear Mr. Layton:

Salutation

Please accept this application for the position of staff accountant at Henley Brothers, Inc. recently posted at Big Sky University. As a result of my work in your controller's office during summers 1999–2001, Janet Stewart, assistant controller, suggested that I seek full-time employment with the company. I will graduate from Big Sky in May 2002 with a B.S. in accounting.

Body

At Big Sky University, I maintained a 3.7 GPA in accounting while working as a volunteer tax preparer and student tutor for 25 hours per week. This record illustrates my commitment to the work ethic, my determination to achieve my goals, and my ability to handle multiple tasks effectively. Big Sky, whose accounting major is communications-intensive, has afforded me the chance to develop strong communication skills as well as solid technical expertise in the fundamentals of accounting. An internship last fall with William Sinclair, CPA, familiarized me with public accounting skills such as financial statement and tax preparation, skills valuable in a corporate environment as well. I believe these skills qualify me to make a positive contribution to Henley Brothers' team.

I would like to present my qualifications in person and will call your office in a week or to two to see if an interview is possible. In the meantime, I can be reached by phone at 809-611-4444. Thank you for considering my application.

Sincerely,

Complimentary Close

Emily A. Baskin

Signature

Enclosure

Figure 6—Sample Cover Letter, Full Block Style

Heading

Emily A. Baskin
1 University Drive
Casper, WY 82001

March 11, 2002

Hunter V. Layton
Human Resources Director
Henley Brothers, Inc.
980 Roosevelt Street
Eden, WY 82926

Inside Address

Dear Mr. Layton:

Salutation

Please accept this application for the position of staff accountant at Henley Brothers, Inc. recently posted at Big Sky University. As a result of my work in the controller's office during summers 1999–2001, Janet Stewart, assistant controller, suggested that I seek full-time employment with the company. I will graduate from Big Sky in May 2002 with a B.S. in accounting.

Body

At Big Sky University, I maintained a 3.7 GPA in accounting while working as a volunteer tax preparer and student tutor for 25 hours per week. This record illustrates my commitment to the work ethic, my determination to achieve my goals, and my ability to handle multiple tasks effectively. Big Sky, whose accounting major is communications-intensive, has afforded me the chance to develop strong communication skills as well as solid technical expertise in the fundamentals of accounting. An internship last fall with William Sinclair, CPA, familiarized me with public accounting skills such as financial statement and tax preparation, skills valuable in a corporate environment as well. I believe these skills qualify me to make a positive contribution to Henley Brothers' team.

I would like to present my qualifications in person and will call your office in a week or to two to see if an interview is possible. In the meantime, I can be reached by phone at 809-611-4444. Thank you for considering my application.

Complimentary Close Sincerely,

Signature Emily A. Baskin

Figure 7—Sample Cover Letter, Modified Block Style

Recommendation for Action Identify the appropriate person at the organization to which you want to apply. Be sure to get the correct spelling of that person's name, the person's title, and full address. Draft your cover letter; proofread carefully.

As with your résumé, have a career counselor, professor, or friend read your cover letter to make suggestions and check for errors. Then, revise and proofread again.

When you are satisfied with your cover letter, sign it, attach it to your résumé with a paper clip, and mail the application in a No. 10 (standard size) envelope.

AN IMPORTANT REMINDER: During the job search, employers will be calling you at the phone numbers you have provided. Be ready to accept these calls in a businesslike manner! If you have a creative, humorous, or otherwise unconventional message on your answering machine or voice mail, change it. If you live with roommates or family members, explain to them how you want to handle calls from potential employers. Always return calls promptly.

If you have not heard from an employer within four weeks of submitting an application, it is appropriate to call and inquire about the status of your application.

PREPARING FOR THE INTERVIEW

Employers hire people who can show they have done their homework, so prepare thoroughly for your interview by finding out all you can about the organization interviewing you and anticipating interview questions (and answers!).

Research the Employer

Your first task is to find out as much as you can about the firm or company where you will be interviewing. Here are some ways to do that:

- *Gather information about the firm or company* and study it carefully. You'll want to show in your interview that you understand the organization's priorities, its strategic direction, its main practice areas, its client base, its emerging markets, its positioning among the competition, and so forth. The organization's annual report can provide this information. Check the World Wide Web to see whether the firm maintains a Web site. If no annual report or Web site exists, consult the organization's brochures and any other literature you can acquire.
- *Research the company and its industry* by reading articles in business publications, professional journals, magazines, and newspapers.
- *Talk with faculty and placement counselors about the firm or company.* Ask about the organization's strengths, about practice trends, and about alumni who have been hired in the last few years.
- *Attend presentations sponsored by the firm or company* where you hope to interview. Talk to the organization's representatives at recruiting sessions and/or professional meetings.
- *Do informational interviews with people who work for the organization.* Ask for their opinions of the company and their advice on interviewing for the job.

- *Consult the organization's Web site, if one exists, for advice on preparing for interviews.* Some firms post sample questions to help interviewees prepare. Or check one of the large multinational public firm's Web sites, even if you are not interviewing there. Each of these firm's Web sites offers tips on interview preparation, and these suggestions may be helpful in the interview you are planning.
- *Prepare several questions of your own.* You can demonstrate that you have done your homework by asking the interviewer intelligent questions about the company. Use the information you have gathered about the company and the industry to frame questions about the company's competitive strategies, emerging markets, and so forth. Anchor each question in specific information to show the interviewer that you are knowledgeable about the organization.

  Examples: Has your company's recent restructuring yielded the kinds of positive changes that were expected?

  How has the company adjusted to its new CEO, after the retirement of Andrew Adams last year?

  Your market entry efforts in Japan have been impressive. Do you foresee continued growth in the Asian sector?

Anticipate Questions, Rehearse Answers

Your next task is to get ready to present yourself as the person best suited for the job. You can do that by anticipating the kinds of questions you may be asked, preparing and practicing answers, and assembling documents that establish your qualifications.

Many employers now use behavioral interviewing techniques to structure job interviews. Behavioral questions are work-based and ask the applicant to link past behavior to behaviors required in the organization conducting the interview. The behavioral interviewer asks applicants to describe past experiences in challenging situations to gauge how they will face similar situations that may arise on the job.

How to Prepare?

Think about all the behaviors that you feel are essential to the job. The more specific you can be about the exact job you're interviewing for, the better prepared you can be to do this. Informational interviewing beforehand helps!

Then, try to think of examples from your past when you exhibited these behaviors. Don't focus on tasks performed such as preparing spreadsheets or answering telephones. Rather, focus on important behaviors such as delegating, scheduling, and organizing. Jot down your thoughts.

Ask yourself the questions on the following list. Think of a response that:

- describes your past behavior
- includes one or more of your positive personal characteristics
- includes one or more of your competencies/skills
- indicates how you might behave in the future in a similar situation

Here are some sample behavior-based questions:

- Tell me about an idea you had for changing the status quo in some situation and what you did with this idea.
- Tell me about a project you initiated and how you did it.
- Describe a situation in which you showed leadership and what resulted from your efforts.
- Describe a situation in which you felt challenged and how you handled it.
- Describe a situation in which you exercised your creativity and talk about the results.
- Describe a situation in which you used interpersonal skills to solve a problem.
- Describe a situation in which you used analytical skills to solve a problem.
- Tell me about a tough decision you had to make and how you handled it.
- Tell me about a time you had to deliver bad news and how you handled it.

Numerous Web sites offer help on preparing for behavior-based interviews. For more information, see:

http://www.collegegrad.com/jobsearch/16-5.shtml

http://www.bsu.edu/students/careers/students/interviewing/intvbbi/

http://rutgers.placementmanual.com/interviewing/interviewing-02.html

Write down your answers, and rehearse them out loud. Then practice, practice, practice. Make an appointment with your college placement office for a mock interview. Placement counselors can give you expert feedback and suggest ways to improve your performance. If this option is not available, have a friend ask you questions, listen to your answers, and offer feedback.

Through your placement office or accounting club, call on outside professionals. Many large firms are willing to send recruiting personnel to colleges and universities to do mock interviews with interested students. Or, ask a local chapter of a professional organization if they have members who would be willing to do one or more mock interviews. Local chapters of state societies of CPAs, the Institute of Management Accountants, the Institute of Internal Auditors, and the Financial Executive Institute usually have committees that work with local colleges and would welcome the opportunity to hold a mock interview session with students.

The important thing is to practice talking about yourself so that you seem natural and relaxed in your interview.

Here are some final tips:

- *Prepare a portfolio that gives evidence of your accomplishments.* Show what you've done by bringing copies of class assignments, projects, papers, spreadsheets, and so forth. Of course, these documents should be error-free! If your professor had marked errors or suggested changes when grading the assignments, be sure to make the corrections and do the revisions before placing them in your portfolio. A simple, two-pocket folder in a dark color will serve the purpose.
- *Make extra copies of your résumé and reference sheet.* You may be asked to interview with more than one person. It is a courtesy to provide copies of your résumé to all

involved. Besides, extra copies give you the chance to focus everybody on the stellar qualifications you've recorded on your résumé!

- *Familiarize yourself with the location of the interview and your route.* Make sure you know exactly where you're going and how long it takes to get there using whatever transportation you plan to take. Get a map if you need to. Drive to the location at the same time of day that the interview is scheduled to determine the length of the trip in traffic. Allow time for getting gas, for traffic jams, even for a flat tire. If you plan to take public transportation, ride to the place on the bus, streetcar, or subway.
- *Plan what you will wear to the interview* (see below). Leave plenty of time to have your clothes laundered and pressed.

DRESSING FOR THE INTERVIEW

Your résumé has gotten you in the door for the interview. Now you have to present yourself as a person who understands the professional world, its customs, and its decorum. You have to present yourself to the employer as a person who will fit in with the organization. The first impression you make is vital, and much of that impression is shaped by how you are dressed.

The professional world of accounting and finance is a conservative one. Although during the past decade or so many organizations relaxed dress codes from "business formal" to "business casual," today's trend is a movement back to business formal. The people who will hire you expect you to appear for your interview appropriately—that is, conservatively—dressed. Once you're hired, they may tell you that more casual dressing is the norm, but DO NOT appear at your interview in anything but your conservative best.

Men should attend interviews dressed as follows:

Dark navy or dark gray business suit, with or without faint pinstripes
White shirt (preferably new), clean and starched, especially at cuffs and collar
Lace-up shoes (Oxfords or wing-tips), in polished black
Belt that matches shoes
Diagonally striped or solid tie (no electric colors or whimsical images)
No earrings, necklaces, bracelets; a watch is fine

Common sense should dictate male grooming:

No strong cologne or aftershave
Clean, trimmed fingernails
Clean hair, freshly cut; no visible gel styling
Clean shaven face; no moustaches, beards, or partial beards

If you smoke, avoid smoking in the hours before your interview, and don't smoke in your interview outfit. (This also applies to women, of course.)

Women should attend interviews dressed as follows:

Dark navy, dark gray, or black business suit, with or without faint pinstripes

Shirt in solid white, ivory, pale blue, or yellow (preferably new, clean and starched, especially at cuffs and collar); a jewel-neck sweater or shell is also acceptable, but a turtleneck is too casual

Skirt should be at least knee-length, not too long

Neutral to dark hose (not black)

Low-heeled pumps if you're tall; otherwise, a medium heel (around 1 1/2 inches); no strappy or platform styles

No flashy or chunky jewelry, no dangling earrings (try small silver, gold, or pearl studs); a simple necklace or strand of pearls; one ring or none; a watch

Again, let common sense dictate grooming:

No strong perfume

Clean, reasonably short fingernails (a clear or neutral nail polish is acceptable); no false nails

Hair in your favorite style, but avoid hiding your face

Minimal makeup: light foundation and a little blush; mascara but little or no eye shadow; a modest, neutral lipstick or gloss (no bright red)

For more information on proper business attire, consult the following Web sites:

http://www.jobweb.org/catapult/guenov/restips.html

http://www.quintcareers.com/dress_for_success.html

http://www.collegegrad.com/book/15-5.shtml

http://www.fordham.edu/cpp/appearance.htm

http://rutgers.placementmanual.com/interviewing/interviewing-03.html

Recommendation for Action Arrange for a mock interview, and wear your interviewing suit. Video- or audio-tape the interview if you can, and ask the interviewer to take notes. After you have completed the mock interview, watch or listen to the tape and listen to your interviewer's critique. Create a list of changes you need to make before your initial interview with a potential employer. These may include résumé or cover letter changes, changes in your dress or appearance, modifications to your handshake or body language, or improvements to the specific answers you gave during the interview.

THE INTERVIEW

If you are interviewing at a large firm or company, the initial interview may be part of a screening process involving a large number of job candidates. In these circumstances, the interviewer's purpose is to identify those applicants who will be invited back for more in-depth interviews. At smaller organizations, hiring decisions may be made on the basis of a single interview. Interviews may be highly structured, following a series of specific questions, or may have little structure at all, with the interviewer simply asking the applicant, "Tell me about yourself." Although no two interviews are alike, the following guidelines are applicable in most interviewing situations:

- *Arrive on time.* That means within a few minutes of the appointment time, no more, no less. If you're late to your interview, you communicate to the interviewer that you can't be on time even for very important business. But, it's also a mistake to be too early. Arriving 20 minutes ahead of time suggests that you're too eager. It may also intrude on the time of the people who will be interviewing you, because someone will have to acknowledge your presence, ask if you'd like coffee, and so forth. If you arrive early, take a walk. Then, show up promptly.
- *Pay attention to your body language.* Our nonverbal communication often says far more than our words, and it's with our body language that we project confidence and competence. Give the interviewer a friendly smile and a strong handshake. Sit comfortably without lounging in your chair. Maintain eye contact with your interviewer(s). (See Figure 8 for more about body language.)

Posture

- Leaning toward the interviewer shows you're interested and engaged
- Folding both arms suggests you're defensive or disagreeing
- Gripping objects like your coat or purse indicates nervousness
- Standing with hands on hips and shoulders back conveys bossiness

Facial Expression and Eye Contact

- Gazing directly at the eye level of the other person indicates confidence and honesty
- Shifty eyes suggest deviousness
- Lack of eye contact suggests that you're lying

Gestures

- Warm gestures—leaning toward people when speaking, facing them directly, smiling, and gesturing expressively
- Cold gestures—hands on hips, slumping, avoiding eye contact, and not smiling
- Nervousness—drumming your fingers, fiddling with objects or jewelry, looking at your watch, scratching

Figure 8—Body Language

Figure 9—Interviewing

- *Express yourself in complete thoughts.* Use proper grammar, and answer questions as logically and clearly as you can. Don't talk too much, however! You don't want to appear long-winded.
- *Remember that you are promoting yourself to the interviewee.* Frame your answers whenever possible to demonstrate your unique talents, strengths, and qualifications for the job. Don't brag, of course, but answer in such a way that your strengths are clarified.
- *Give concrete evidence to support general statements.* If you describe yourself as a team player, for example, support that assertion by describing a situation in which your teamwork had productive results.
- *Demonstrate your understanding of the employer's business, goals, and corporate culture.* Use all that research you've done on the organization. As you answer questions, talk specifically about what you could bring to projects, initiatives, and developments in which you know the company is engaged.
- *Never blame anyone or anything* else for a less-than-outstanding grade or other deficiency on your résumé. Address the subject directly, emphasize your strong points, and speak about yourself in a positive way.
- *Listen carefully to everything the interviewer says,* whether it is a question or an answer to a question you have asked. Careful listening will allow you to pick up on points your interviewer makes, to extend discussion about those points, and to generate further questions. Showing that you're a good listener is just as important as showing that you are articulate and well-prepared.
- *If you do not understand a question, ask the interviewer to clarify it.* Trying to respond to an unclear question will probably result in an unsatisfactory answer.
- *Ask the questions you have prepared and any others that you have formulated during the course of the interview.* But, don't ask about salary in an initial interview. A salary offer will be made when (or after) an offer of employment is made. Feel free to ask, however,

about employee training and career paths within the company. If the interviewer asks you about your salary requirements, explain that you are more interested in the "job fit," the opportunities for advancement, and other matters at this stage than you are in a specific target salary.

- *At the conclusion of the interview, thank the interviewer and offer another smile and firm handshake.* Ask for a business card if the interviewer has not given you one. You will use it for the follow-up note.

A Few Words About Business Meals. . .

Often, when you are interviewing for a job, you will be invited to have lunch with one or more of your interviewers. If you are visiting the organization for an entire day, as is sometimes the case in second interviews, you may be asked to both lunch and dinner. At these meals, your interviewers aren't just giving you a free lunch: They want to see how you conduct yourself at the dining table because a lot of business is done over meals.

If those table manners your mother drilled into you have become a bit rusty, use the following tips to look good at your interview meal.

<u>As the Meal Begins:</u>

- Place your purse or briefcase on the floor or on an empty chair.
- Turn off your cell phone.
- Unfold your napkin and put it in your lap. (Don't tuck it into your neckline!)
- When ordering from the menu, follow your host's lead. Either ask the host what he or she recommends or choose from the mid-price range. Only order an appetizer or dessert if others do, too.
- Don't order alcohol.
- Avoid messy foods that are awkward to eat: long thin pasta, sandwiches, food with gravy, chicken on the bone, fish with bones, shrimp with tails.
- After ordering, close the menu and put it beside you.
- If in a self-serve restaurant, take your food off the tray to eat it.
- Wait for your host to begin eating unless you're at a banquet dinner. In that case, wait until a few others begin.

<u>Handling Cutlery</u> Although place settings at informal meals are relatively simple (fork to left of plate, spoon and knife to right; salad plate above fork; water glass above knife), settings at formal dinners and banquets can be bewildering. The last thing you need to worry about at a business dinner is how to use your cutlery. If you study the following guidelines before you go, you'll be fine. Figure 10 illustrates a formal place setting.

A Napkin
B Luncheon plate
C Soup (or other first course plate) on a liner plate
D Bread and butter plate with butter knife
E Water glass
F Wine glass
G Luncheon fork
H Knife
I Teaspoon
J Soup spoon

Figure 10—Standard Table Setting

A few simple rules apply to the use of cutlery and glassware:

- There are two acceptable ways to handle a knife and fork. In both methods, the knife is held in the right hand for cutting and the fork is held in the left to position the food. In the American method, the knife is placed on the plate (blade inward) after the food is cut and the fork transferred to the right hand to convey food to the mouth, tines pointing upward. In the European method, the knife remains in the right hand and the left hand holds the fork to convey the food to the mouth, tines pointing downward.
- Whichever method you use, do not cut more food at one time than you can eat in a bite or two. Be sure to put cutlery down on your plate in between bites and courses. Do not gesture with your cutlery.
- If soup is served, move the spoon away from yourself to convey it to your mouth. Never slurp the soup. In between bites and when you are finished, place the soup spoon on the plate under the soup bowl; do not leave it sticking out of the bowl.
- As bread and butter are passed, put the bread on your bread-and-butter plate. Use your butter knife to take a small portion of butter and place it on that plate as well. Then, butter your bread with the butter knife.
- If your host orders wine, wait to drink until all diners' glasses have been filled (unless you're at a banquet; then wait until several people have been served). Hold the wine glass by the stem.
- When you have finished eating, place your fork and knife together, diagonally across the right side of your plate with the knife on the outside of the fork. The knife blade should point inward.
- Use your teaspoon to stir sugar and/or cream in your coffee after the meal. Then, place the spoon on the saucer under the cup.

During the Meal: Other Tips

- Maintain good posture; bring your food to your mouth and don't lean over to take bites.
- Keep your elbows off the table. Although a bit of gentle leaning on your forearm or hand is okay, it's better to keep your hands in your lap.
- Keep your voice down; no loud talking.
- Use your napkin to blot or dab, never to wipe.
- If food gets caught in your teeth, don't pick or use a toothpick. Go to the restroom.
- If you must leave the table, leave your napkin on the chair and excuse yourself.
- If someone spills, offer your napkin, but get the server, and let him or her take over.
- If food falls off your plate, pick it up with a utensil. If you drop a fork, ask for another.
- Never talk with your mouth full or chew with your mouth open. Take small bites.

At the End of the Meal

- Don't stack your dishes or lift your plate to hand it to the server.
- Don't smoke.
- Don't ask for a doggie bag.
- Always thank the host for the meal.
- Leave your napkin on the table next to your plate, not on your chair.

Numerous sources on business etiquette and dining are available on the Internet. For more information, see:

http://www.bsu.edu/students/careers/students/interviewing/dining/

http://www.fsu.edu/~success/tips/dining.htm

http://www.scu.edu/careercenter/resources/pdf/Pro_social_Etiquette.pdf

FOLLOWING UP AFTER THE INTERVIEW

Thank-You Notes

Send the interviewer a thank-you note within 48 hours of the interview. Although some career professionals suggest handwritten notes, you are always safe with a clean word-processed letter. You can adopt a more personal tone in the thank-you note than you did in the cover letter, because you are now acquainted with your reader.

In addition to thanking the interviewer for his or her time, you may want to comment on something you learned during the interview or refer to a key point that arose in the conversation. You should reiterate your interest in the position, and comment briefly on your qualifications to fill it. The thank you note in Figure 11 offers a model using the full block style.

Brian T. Randolph
131 Laguna Way
Albany, TX 76430

April 23, 2002

Kurt M. Higgins
Controller
Global Oil Exploration
3452 Desert Sky Avenue
Dallas, TX 75265

Dear Mr. Higgins:

Thank you for the opportunity to meet with you yesterday to discuss the staff accountant position at Global Oil Exploration, Inc.

It was interesting to see the similarities between the accounting operations of Global Oil and AT&T, where I have worked as an intern for the past nine months. I was quite impressed to hear of the efficiency and speed with which Global recently implemented its SAP software system. Successful implementation of such a complex system speaks well for the people who work for your company. Our conversation affirmed my belief that I can bring valuable accounting, computer, and communication skills and experience to the job.

I am enclosing the article we discussed about the CPA WebTrust program for company Web sites. I think you will find it interesting.

Thanks once again for the interview. I look forward to discussing the position further.

Sincerely,

Brian T. Randolph

Enclosure

Figure 11—Sample Interview Thank-You Letter

Supplemental Materials

If the interviewer has requested any materials (additional references, work samples) send them along with the thank-you note—that is, within 48 hours. If the employer has requested transcripts, ask your college registrar's office to send them out immediately, and let the employer know that they are on the way.

Further References

If you have a reference or contact who has influence with the company, you may want to ask that person to call the interviewer and put in a good word for you. Use your judgment before making such a request, however. If the interviewer seemed very interested in your application, he or she will probably be receptive to an extra push. If, however, the interviewer was hard to read, firm about the screening procedures, or explicit about the method of checking references, you should simply leave matters in the interviewer's hands.

Calling to Inquire

If two weeks or more have elapsed since the interview and you have not heard from the employer, it is appropriate to call and ask about the status of your application. Simply do so politely, and express your continued interest in the job.

If you have received another job offer but want this one, call the interviewer and explain that you need to make a decision. If the screening process is still under way, the interviewer may at least be able to tell you when offers will be made.

Accepting the Job

If you are offered the position for which you interviewed and you accept it verbally, it is a courtesy to send a brief letter of acceptance as well (see Figure 12).

Brian T. Randolph
131 Laguna Way
Albany, TX 76430

April 23, 2002

Kurt M. Higgins
Controller
Global Oil Exploration
3452 Desert Sky Avenue
Dallas, TX 75265

Dear Mr. Higgins:

I am happy to accept the position of staff accountant in your controller's office. As you know, Global Oil has been my first choice throughout the job search process.

I have completed the forms you enclosed in your letter of offer, and I look forward to seeing you on Monday, June 13.

Sincerely,

Brian T. Randolph

Figure 12—Sample Acceptance Letter

Declining the Job

If you are offered the position for which you interviewed and want to decline it, you should do so in a brief letter as well (see Figure 13). The purpose of this letter is to maintain goodwill with the employer, because you may wish to reapply for a position at some future time or you may find yourself coming in business contact with employees of the company. Therefore, take care to reject the offer politely and to offer a plausible reason for declining.

Brian T. Randolph
131 Laguna Way
Albany, TX 76430

April 23, 2002

Kurt M. Higgins
Controller
Global Oil Exploration
3452 Desert Sky Avenue
Dallas, TX 75265

Dear Mr. Higgins:

Thank you for your offer of an accounting position at Global Oil. Global is one of the most dynamic companies in the oil business today, and it would be a privilege to be a part of your team.

I have also received an offer, however, from Texas Instruments, where I worked as an intern last year. The relationships I have already begun to build there, coupled with a very attractive financial package, have led me to accept Texas Instruments' offer.

I appreciate your interest in me and regret that I cannot accept your generous offer.

Sincerely,

Brian T. Randolph

Figure 13—Sample Letter Declining Offer

CONCLUSION

Now, more than ever before, accounting majors have a wealth of career options to pursue. Starting early, researching these options, targeting internships and summer jobs that appeal to you, preparing a functional résumé and cover letter, and interviewing skillfully are the first steps to turning these options into a successful career. Career-related volunteer work, along with internships and summer jobs, are the steps that turn a solid functional résumé into a powerful sales tool to use upon graduation.

This guidebook takes you step-by-step through the career search process, from learning about the profession as a freshman to landing the job you want after college graduation. Follow the recommendations for action throughout the guide to launch your successful accounting career.